The Rainbow Factor

7 Steps to Life Engagement

By Frances Tolton

EsteemWorld Publications
United Kingdom

The Rainbow Factor – 7 Steps to Life Engagement
Copyright © 2010 by Frances Tolton

ISBN: 978-1-907011-00-9

Published in the United Kingdom by:
EsteemWorld Publications

British Library Cataloguing In Publication Data
A Record of this Publication is available from the British
Library.

For further information or permission, contact:
EsteemWorld Publications
United Kingdom
E-mail: info@esteemworldpublications.com
Website: www.esteemworldpublications.com

Printed in Great Britain for EsteemWorld Publications

The Rainbow Factor

7 Steps to Life Engagement

For my parents Joan & Donal – thank you for so many "Happy Days"

"I read and walked for miles at night along the beach, writing bad blank verse and searching endlessly for someone wonderful who would step out of the darkness and change my life. It never crossed my mind that that person could be me." Anna Quindlin

The Rainbow Factor

Foreword

This book could change your life. I know it because I've lived it.

Having come through years of reading experiences, from secrets to circles and miraculous fix-all philosophies of how to get rich quick, I created *The Rainbow Factor.* This is a practical process to get you beyond the borders of possibility, to reality by engaging with your goals.

The Rainbow Factor is a process of engagement which brings out the inner magic in each of us. In other words, it summons up your own personal power to achieve. *The Rainbow Factor* is for anyone who has been dreaming but not really waking up to the reality of their dreams.

It is for anyone who has been setting those goals but often finishing just short of achievement. It is for anyone who has been knocking on the door of the universe but finding that nobody seems to be home.

We all have the power to create magic in our lives. We just need to know how, and the most exciting and rewarding way is through Life Engagement. Whether we are seeking personal or business achievement, work-life balance, fulfilment in relationships, or if we just want to find and re-energize our life's passion, success lies in engagement!

I dedicate this book and all of its magic to the many people who have helped me to realise my power. To Joan and Donal, my inspirational parents who were, and are, my guides in life. To my husband, Liam, whose eternal belief in me drives me onwards, and to the many, many inspirited colleagues and mentors I have met all over the world. You are all wizards!

Acknowledgements

Many people have helped in the creation of this book, and to all of them I express my heartfelt thanks.

- To my husband, Liam, for his constant encouragement and great cooking during the writing of this book.
- To Jeri Reilly, my editor, whose beautiful personality and guidance made this writing a sheer joy.
- To Tony & Vanessa Geoghegan, photographers extraordinaire for whom nothing is too much trouble.
- To the amazingly talented Susan Tomelty for the wonderful musical creation which is "Luisne" – the theme to this book on audio.
- To Ann Harrington for her constant support in finding everything she could about rainbows and her help in the research for this book.

- To my dear friends Mirjana, Gary & Jim for their unbridled generosity in sharing their passion for sailing.
- To Brian & Sangeeta Mayne for their friendship, mentoring and pure authenticity.
- To Nick Imoru at EsteemWorld Publications for his endless patience and emailed blessings.

Thank you all from the bottom of my heart!

Contents

Introduction

The Rainbow Factor
Finding the Wizard
Within

Over the coming chapters you will learn 7 steps that will unlock your inner potential and turn it into immediate goal centered activity.

The wonderful news about *The Rainbow Factor* is that this process requires nothing more than a clear head, a positive frame of mind and the passion to see your goal through to its achievement.

There are lots of pretty difficult books out there about goals and goal setting, some suggesting that to truly succeed, you need a fairly spectacular background and training in personal development. However, if I were to offer any direction on desirable traits, or personal competencies to engage with *The Rainbow Factor* process, it would be to have done some serious living in this world, and to be at least a willing and if possible, positive participant in that living. Since you have been attracted in some way towards this book and what it offers, I would say that you are already eminently qualified to embark on this journey. So, welcome to *The Rainbow Factor.*

What is it with Rainbows?

The rainbow is one of the most ancient of human symbols, its origins stretching back to biblical times and beyond. In the book of Genesis, we read how God said to Noah, "I have set my bow in the clouds, and it will be the sign of the covenant between me and the earth." Numerous other references remind us of the importance and nature of this covenant which is forever now embedded in the rainbow.

The scientists among us will perhaps prefer the more Newtonian analysis of this amazing phenomenon. In

1666, Sir Isaac Newton (1643-1727) demonstrated that sunlight is actually made up of many colours which when combined, seem white to the human eye. When the light from these different colours passes through air or water it is refracted by varying amounts, and forms what we see in the sky as a beautifully coloured rainbow. As early as the 1500s René Descartes (1596-1650) and Willebrord Snell (1580-1626) determined how a ray of light is bent, or refracted, as it crosses areas of different densities such as air and water and forms the bow shape.

This allows us to see seven colours - red, orange, yellow, green, blue, indigo, and violet - as I was taught in school to remember by "Roy of York gave battle in vain". However, there is a wonderful analogy here in the rainbow because just as our lives are symphonies of experience carrying us through pain and joy, the rainbow is also a symphony of colour from red to violet and beyond the colours that the eye can see.

Author, Donald Ahrens describes the rainbow as "one of the most spectacular light shows observed on earth".

In myth and legend, the rainbow represents that eternally possible or elusive pot of gold that lies at its end. It symbolizes hope and imagination or simply a lost sense of wonder. That same wonder that was once the sheer life surge of civilisation but is now grossly replaced by a technological torrent of instantly accessible knowledge and answers, which is gradually closing the aperture of wonder.

The vision of a rainbow is covenant, and it is hope. It serves as a constant reminder that having come through the storm, mystery and beauty still exist and are freely available. The rainbow is a lesson for life. Just as we need to experience pain to truly appreciate joy, so too, to see a rainbow we need to have experienced both rain and sunshine.

Whichever version of the origin of this wonderful, natural phenomenon we prefer - the biblical or the scientific, the rainbow remains one of the most beautiful, mysterious and yes, magical manifestations on earth. There are few who do not wonder at its appearance in that watery sunlight after a shower, and it never fails to draw the human eye towards its magical presence.

In *The Rainbow Factor*, we will use the powerful symbolism of the rainbow to restart our lives, rekindle our dreams and re-energize our goals. Each of the seven letters and colours will represent for us an important step in becoming authors of our own success. The seven letters in the word *Rainbow* will form the basis and structure for a proactive daily process for engaging with life's challenges on every level.

Sometimes we find ourselves letting go of our vision or dismissing our dreams. Our sacrifice of that goal is often because the time is presumably not right, or the world presents a big enough case for us to just not "go for it" and abandon our ambition. That promotion at work, the decision to improve our health and well being, the house move, the writing of that book, the trip that you will someday make or the garden that each season reminds us of the repeated promises of attention, all speak volumes on the price of the sacrifice. Even the courageous commitment to do what you really love to do in life and not what you have to, are all there to be activated by our personal commitment to actually doing something about it.

Despite our significant education in personal development and the subsequent raising of our awareness, many people still lack the vital keys which unlock that door to success. Today, that ends. Today you start again to make a difference to your life by learning how to move from just thinking and dreaming to actually doing and achieving.

Chapter 1

Creating
The Rainbow Factor
Mindset

"Life isn't about finding yourself. Life is about creating yourself".
- George Bernard Shaw

For any of the challenges of our lives, positioning is everything. In other words, we need to get ourselves lined up and prepared for action. We can all witness to some life experience when being prepared and in the right mind set proved crucial to our success or achievement. Equally so, we can all lay claim to those "only if" scenarios when we came within the proverbial hair's breadth of achieving the goal or realizing the dream, but were robbed of that moment of triumph because we failed to adequately prepare.

This is not to take from the power of the spontaneous act or gut instinct that proves its authentic basis in delivery. However, there are many situations when a little time taken to plan and to focus our thinking will reel in and secure our success.

To achieve any life learning, to arrive at any insight, we need to position our thinking and our lives in preparation for the outcome.

Successful athletes spend many gruelling years leading their bodies and minds to the place where their true greatness resides.

You are invited to become an athlete in your own personal development and to enter into training for your own impending greatness.

As you begin the first chapter of this book, I invite you to make a promise to yourself - that this is a new beginning for you and your life as an achiever.

Once you have made that vital agreement with yourself, there are three empowering principles that will support you in joyfully engaging with the magic of your destiny.

Principle 1- Live in an Authentic Mindset

We live in the "positive generation"– pretty good I guess! Our lives are punctuated by reminders to "think positive". Over recent years, we have been bombarded by a wave of messages to be positive, to such an extent that to think any other way suggests an impeded mind and to submit to the experience of "a bad day" sets off the alarm bells. I suggest that this seratonin-drenched popular philosophy can bypass the peaceful simplicity of a genuine positive thought, which is within the inherent capacity of every human being.

These are the thoughts and feelings that don't necessitate any "tuning in" or calibration of our mental antennae to attract some mysterious universal signalling system.

These are not the products of the modern day on-tap mindset which is turned on and off depending on what life presents us with and which demands no real human commitment to consciousness.

Instead, these thoughts and feelings can be experienced and enjoyed for what they are in their basic simplicity. *The Rainbow Factor* asks us to enter into a mindset sparked by a conscious decision to connect with the simpler and authentic things of life – the wonder of yet another morning, the sweet taste of berries, wonderful memories or laughter that makes your stomach hurt.

To enter this mindset demands more than the guru laden book shelf or the daily dose of affirmations taken religiously with the drive to work.

To create the authentic mindset we need to stop, extract ourselves from the frantic pace of our lives and consciously give nature and experience permission to enter through the doors of our senses. It takes the ability to step into life and take our chances with both the rapturous and the despairing. It is the capacity to reap a full harvest of experience which grounds our very presence and sustains us beyond the present moment.

Through this we achieve the groundedness of being, which is a stranger to the "dip-in" mentality of some new age "positive thinking" philosophies.

Once we discover the authentic mindset, we nourish it with loving attention so that it can become deeply ingrained and become a way of life – not a secret but a reality. Living this authentic mindset provides a powerful springboard from which we can reach out, dive into the possibilities of life and position ourselves to engage with our dreams.

Actions to take to discover and nurture your Authentic Mindset

- *Get close to nature*. A great idea is to create a "nature taster" menu and set out to experience as many aspects of nature as possible until you find those aspects which make your senses tingle. Then go do those things. Your menu could include a trip to a lake, listening to birdsong, wondering at a night sky, swimming in the sea or spending time with animals and on it goes. For me there is nothing can match time with my dogs at a nearby lake and the sheer exhilaration of sailing with the sun, the wind and the spray in my face. Once you find your "fix" – give it space in your life.

- *Spend time with people you love* –
  If you only do this "when you have time", after all the other stuff, well then you are losing out on one of the most vibrant parts of living an authentic life. We live in an age in which contact is high and connection is low. We have a plethora of "off the hook" contact systems, the use of which have become a default position in our lives. This "text don't talk" and the "leave a message" age deprives us every day of the joy and authenticity of living face-to-face, communicating by voice

and having that heart-to-heart. So increase and deepen your connection – spend time whenever you can and be conscious of when quick-fix contact is depriving you of the love and connection associated with the person-to-person experience.

- *Identify and live your passions!* – be clear about what you are doing with your life. Identify those things or activities that you love to do and that make you feel fresh and alive and go do them!

This takes courage and commitment. In the summer of 2008, I was in my local bookshop checking out the Personal Development section. I reached to the top shelf to take down a book when the book just beside it slipped out and fell on my head. Over the following weeks I realised this was the best bang on the head I ever got. The book was called *The Passion Test* by Janet Bray Attwood and Chris Attwood, and it started me on a journey that eight months later led me to Toronto, Canada, to work on becoming a certified

Passion Test facilitator. I returned with a new clarity about my own life's passions and I am now regularly helping others to discover theirs. My advice – go get the book and do the passion test. It is the one test you can never fail and you will discover what you really want in life. Then live it, because you can never live an authentic life if you are not living your passions. Remember that those passions can range from the simplest activities or interests to more challenging and perhaps even life-changing occupations. While helping people to identify their passions I have worked with individuals whose passion is to simply read or study, spend time in their gardens or even just sit down and relax in their own home, activities which they have stopped doing due to their busy lives. Others have a passion for dancing, theatre, or even one guy has a passion for flying small aeroplanes but he just doesn't get to it anymore. My own passions range from time with my husband, to writing and speaking, being with my three boxer dogs and sailing. I make sure that these passions have a place in my life. So too, you can live your passions. Find out what they are and go for it!

* * *

Even if your circumstances make it difficult for you to spend time living your passions, decide to find a way to live them as much as you can. By engaging with even a small amount of what you love will light up your whole being. It is important to also mention that your passions can lie in your work or career. To find the career that energizes you and fills you with joy is the ultimate professional achievement. Once again, identify it and go towards it so that it can play a key role in helping you to live your authentic life.

Principle 2 - Live in Abundance

Positioning for *The Rainbow Factor* invites us to live in abundance and not in excess. Sometimes it can be hard to balance the scales of life between a sense of abundance and the ever increasing mentality of excess that engulfs our world.

Be conscious, and realize that the universe in its grand generosity showers us with abundance while the material world delivers excess in extraordinary volumes. For many, "super-size me" has become the catch-cry of our physical, mental and spiritual lives.

Obesity has become a significant health issue even for children, and our minds are packed to capacity with information. Even on a spiritual level, we are experiencing a glut of belief systems many of which serve to confuse and block the simple yet powerful abundance of true everyday values like loving one's neighbour.

Western lifestyle supports excess, and as a consequence, continents starve and the earth creaks under a gigantic weight of waste. The outcome is a convenient confusion between abundance and excess. Yet all the while the universe steeps us in its healing abundance and pours relief into the open wounds of an ailing earth. We are offered another way - an alternative. There is a way of life where the durable replaces the disposable in a world of abundance.

You will best engage with *The Rainbow Factor* if you are able to recognize the intrinsic abundance in every experience. Even in the most painful and tragic circumstances, there is a significant generosity, even if it is merely the hope that with time, the anguish will heal and our spirits will be lifted.

In making that shift to a clearer understanding of true abundance, we can be assured that every one of us can make a difference by the way we live our lives. We will know that the action of even one person can truly contribute to changing the world, by striving to live in abundance and not in excess. This doesn't mean that you should feel guilty about having the goods of the world. The secret is in knowing why, and in what quantity. In other words, understanding the difference between what is abundant or excessive. When deciding to acquire anything in life, ask yourself the question, "why am I doing this?" If you think I'm being a little harsh here, just go check the amount of "stuff" you possess that you rarely use, wear, or even look at. We've all done it. We've all given into the two for the price of one of something it takes a year to use anyway and which ends up in the garbage by the time you get to it because it has past its sell-by date or gone out of fashion. Whether we like it or not, this is excess, along with the tons of food wasted in restaurants every night or the exorbitant price paid for goods, just because a company has employed some really smart marketing executive who convinces us that it's worth it. We all need to get real!

Abundance however, means living life without that "over done it" feeling. It is the appropriate, the right amount, even the "free"! It is being conscious of our decisions to acquire possessions, eat food and use the resources of the earth with respect and gratitude. It is living our lives responsibly and with true generosity so that the gifts of life yield a sense of joy as opposed to overindulgence.

Ways to let abundance into your life:
- ***Start your day in gratitude*** – not a new concept I admit, but ever as powerful. The moment you open your eyes in the morning, give thanks for life, who you are and what you have, however great or small. Call into your day the best the universe has in store for you and commit to using it with respect in the best way you can.

Honour your life as a place of abundance and you will open your heart to more.

- **_Add to someone else's life every day_** - and never let a day go by without leaving behind a legacy of kindness. Greet people on the street, tell people how brilliant they are, share positive thoughts, and help someone to laugh. One of my favourites is when I arrive at a hotel and get to my room, I call the receptionist and thank them for the beautiful room – I always seem to get a beautiful room! There is no end to the ways we can spread abundance by the tiny and thoughtful practices of generosity and gratitude that have no choice but to flow both ways. Be aware of the messages you send to people and make sure that every time you communicate, you enhance somebody's life.

- **_Be "upgradeable" in life and expect it to happen._**
  Live every day in your best self and be prepared for minor and major miracles. Forget that old stitched-in message of un-deservedness.

Start today, stand and open your arms wide and say – *"I am open to every piece of good luck that can come my way. If the world wants to treat me, I'm ready, and may I bump straight into my miracles"!* Remember, your natural state is success and abundance and never let an opportunity pass you by unless you have a good reason to turn down the generosity of this abundant universe. And when you have done all of this – turn it all around and do it for someone else. Herein lies true abundance.

Principle 3 - Believe you are Deserving

In 1998, I was invited to speak at a conference in Puerta Vallarta, Mexico. This experience initiated an insatiable thirst for learning about my own and, in turn, others' personal development. From that year onwards, I found myself taking every opportunity to travel and learn with people from different countries and with diverse ways of thinking.

Though now commercialized, Puerta Vallarta, behind its efforts to cater for the tourist, possesses a deep and enduring culture evidenced by remnants of Mayan architecture and achievement. I was in the company of a group of business people exploring the topic of spirituality in the workplace, a concept not regularly visited in the boardrooms of our western organisations. For some in our group who came from the corporate world, it represented some kind of new age thinking which had every chance of undermining the staunch pillars of business. However, there were the enlightened few who believed that far from undermining business, spirituality in the workplace in the form of personal development was the gateway to building potential in business.

On one of the days of the conference, Juan, a fellow delegate invited a small group of us to his home high in the mountains of Jalisco. On arrival we were received and welcomed in a true sense of joy at our visit. The family home was decorated with the most amazing art, all produced by Juan's two sisters. One of my colleagues remarked on the beauty of a picture which hung in the central room in the house.

Immediately, Carmelita, the artist, reached for the picture and handed it to my colleague, insisting with a huge smile that she have it. The generosity and joy of giving away this beautiful piece of art shone through her whole body. Carmelita was amazed when my colleague looked at her and said, "Oh my goodness, you are so kind but I could never take this. It is far too beautiful". Carmelita looked kindly at her and said, "No hay nada mas bonita que la persona", which translates as "there is nothing more beautiful than a person".

Seeing ourselves as deserving doesn't always come easily in a world that promotes non-personal beauty, as opposed to that deeper beauty that emerges from the soul and is ever enduring and deserving.
This was the tangible energy in Carmelita's offering. The person who fails to recognise this in themselves will forever see the possessions or experiences of life as beautiful, and themselves as undeserving.

So how can we address this limiting self perception that propels us away from our sense of deserving self? Well, get yourself back in first place. As people, we have succumbed to being in second place. Technological advances claim to bring us closer together. However a by-product of this has been to sever many of the sustaining links we rely on for having a sense of human family and, in turn, a sense of self. Developing a sense of self and, in particular, that sense of deserving-self, depends hugely on strong, direct and positive human connections.

We human beings carry a sensual ability to build and empower the sense of deserving self in ourselves and those around us. We all need regular doses of encouragement and reassurance by the spoken words and the physical touch of those around us. This is our primary life support system and it cannot be substituted by the communication technologies which now command a primary space in our daily lives.

As we experience this torrent of communication technology our lives are seas of impersonal messages created by impersonal systems and the rapid growth of on-line communication has made these secondary forms of communication our first language.

Our busy fingers scurry over cell phone keys, executives email their colleagues who are two metres away and the world is awash with unchecked recorded messages and communication tools which claim to connect us but in reality serve to widen the gap between people.

Though strides in communication technologies have enabled us to excel in our efficiencies and break the time and space barriers of contact, these advances do not hold the compelling nature of person-to-person contact and taking the time to truly connect. We are losing the wonderful opportunities to sensually affect other people and instead of that "first issue" wave of excitement, heartfelt congratulations, undiluted praise or regret, we receive and deliver "late edition" timed out messages that make it just before the bleep. Remember that feeling of surprised energy at personally delivered good news or the gratitude for the opportunity to sympathise with a friend or colleague in need?

Whatever happened to calling someone, walking to a colleague's desk or popping in to a neighbour? Every day another system is put in place that diminishes human connection.

In business, customer care has suffered hugely because of the reduction of person to person service. How many times have we just given up on a call because there are too many hoops to jump through in order to just speak to a real person?

Sure, we all need to benefit from progress but let's get the order right! Let's put people first again and use these technologies as a support and not as a first option. For me, the greatest communication inventions are those that can bring someone on the other side of the world into my office or living room and enables me to see and talk to them! It's wonderful! - because they are on the other side of the world, but not down the road or two desks away.

We need people to show us, tell us, and remind us "personally" that we are good and deserving human beings, and to let us know from a business perspective, that as customers, we are actually important enough for someone to afford us the courtesy of speaking to us.

Actions to Help You Feel More Deserving

Inject more opportunities for person-to-person contact. This will reignite that life-giving force of really connecting which increases our sense of self as well as inviting others to do the same. When it comes to communicating, stop and choose a means that will yield most value and life for both parties. Speed of contact can often tempt us to choose the easiest, as opposed to the best way.

It may not always be as convenient to call around, pick up the phone or take the time to write a letter, but by choosing to take the time to make the most personal contact you can, you deepen your connection to the other person. Save your texts and emails for the punctuation of life and take the time to talk and connect personally whenever you can.

> ➢ Write letters by hand to family and friends. When you hand write, you slow down the brain so that you can savour the real message you are sending.

> ➢ Seek out opportunities to praise and lift others – they in turn will lift you and build your sense of self deserving.

> ➢ Treat yourself on achievement because you deserve it.

> ➢ Tell yourself regularly that you do deserve all the wonderful things that life offers and that you are open to receive them.

> ➢ When you receive, celebrate and be grateful knowing that all is rightfully yours.

> ➢ Live your life as if you deserve it!

> ➢ Be ever grateful for the power to receive and care for mother earth.

Finally there are three vehicles which will activate and sustain your personal development as you engage with *The Rainbow Factor.*

These are three practical pieces of preparation which will support your efforts.

1 – Create Personal Power Time

Commit to a chosen time every day to work on your *Rainbow Factor.* This can be as little as fifteen minutes but should be totally dedicated to you. Choose your best time of day, when you are most likely to be able to relax, think about your life, identify the goals you want to set and visualise your achievements. Turn off your phone and be ready to resist any disturbance during this period.

I have two favourite *"power times",* first thing in the morning and between five and six in the evening. There is little to equal the sheer peace of early mornings in summer when it's just me and the birds. I equally treasure that lovely evening time in autumn and winter when the light begins to depart the earth and leaves that trail of scorched sky in its wake.

I admit that I was one of those people who just wouldn't take that time out for me.

However, I started with twenty minutes a day and now if my "power time" is anything less than one hour per day, I feel cheated. Just before going to sleep is also of course a wonderful time as your subconscious is hungry for your positive thoughts and eager to get cracking on your goals.

2 – Create a Personal Power Space

Choose a location where you will work on your *Rainbow Factor*. It may be in your house, at your office or outdoors. Once it is conducive to your growth and enjoyment, this location will become your special place. Try if possible to choose a space which reflects who you are. Think about surrounding yourself with as many symbols of your personal achievements as possible. Typical examples are photos of memorable events, certificates, or memorabilia from any travels you have done. Include symbols of activities that make you feel positive - favourite books, pictures etc and most important of all, a comfortable cosy place to sit. Get yourself a good journal and pen with which you will work on your goals. You may want to have some of your favourite music available to you to play on occasion or some motivational material which focuses your mind. Over the years I have built up a collection of audio books which I find inspirational and really helpful in focusing my thinking on success.

I include a list for you at the back of this book. Treat yourself as I do, to a daily 15-30 minutes of reading or listening to your favourite authors and connecting your learning and enjoyment to your goals.

A few years ago, I built a beautiful wooden cabin as my personal power space. It has my favourite chair, and as I sit there, I am surrounded by my favourite books, the artwork I have collected over the years and my collection of miniature elephants. I have decorated this space so that it is most definitely my favourite place to be. I also invite my three dogs to join me as they are my great de-stressors in life.

When you deliberately create your personal power space, you will sense and be comfortable in your own positive and empowering energy. It will flow from those most cherished and joyful life experiences represented all around you.

3 – Create your Personal Power Insulators

Your Personal Power Insulators are your chosen means of protecting yourself against negative thinking and the temptation to abandon your dreams. Choose them and practice them every day. In turn they will sustain your power to succeed by giving you something to reach for when you are in doubt.

Your Power Insulators will be physical, mental or spiritual defence mechanisms with which you engage when necessary. Their practice should become a conscious and unconscious behaviour when you feel your success is threatened by negative thinking, self-doubt or outside influences such as the opinions of other people.

Physical Insulators

A physical insulator is a physical reaction to negativity and doubt. Examples are, physically moving away from threatening and negative situations, people or environments that undermine your resolve. You may be speaking to someone about your plans when they start reminding you of how many people have failed in the past trying to do exactly what you are trying to do now. Move away from them!

Remember, there is always something to be learned from someone's past efforts but just because they may not have succeeded doesn't mean you won't. The difference this time is - it's YOU. Employ your physical insulator and move on. Get talking to people who will admire your efforts, offer you positive and constructive advice and encourage you onwards. Stay physically away from doomsayers. We've already explored the idea of your power space which is a really effective physical insulator. Other examples of physical insulators are using physical things to remind you of your success.

I have a client who when losing weight bought seven little coloured pebbles to represent roughly the seven kilos in a stone of weight. She also bought 4 larger beautiful pieces of coloured quartz crystal rock to represent the four stones in weight she wanted to lose. Every time she lost a kilo in weight, she presented herself with one of the small pretty pebbles until she lost just over seven kilos and then presented herself with one of the beautiful quartz rocks to mark her achievement. She placed her physical reminders in a prominent place in her kitchen where she could regularly see them when eating and these became her physical insulators against the temptation to eat unhealthy food. She has already collected three of her quartz rocks!

The conscious activity of creating conducive environments for your personal progress, making practical plans which support and enable your efforts, and manifesting in material ways your goal driven activity, all represent the power of physical insulators in your personal development.

One of my own favourite physical insulators is my dream box. It's a beautiful mother of pearl box in which I keep pictures and little symbols that remind me of my dreams and goals. I of course keep it in my cabin. Sometimes, I come across a little charm or toy and it says something to me about those great works in progress. Of course the added benefit is the visual nature of my dream box, the contents of which serve as visualisations of the future.

Mental Insulators

Mental insulators are mental reactions to negativity and doubt. They are positive thoughts which help to support and strengthen your resolve. They will help you resist sowing the seeds of doubt in your thinking and thereby undermining your resolve. Mental insulators demand the ability to think clearly and with focus when your power over your goals and ambitions is challenged.

People who rely on mental insulators spend time building the strength of that mind muscle which supports them in maintaining their pure clarity of focus and personal resolve.

The most important mental insulator is the ability to deal with the "little voice" in your head which tells you that you can't, and supports that claim with what look like good reasons. Dealing with your little voice is the most important skill in building strong and reliable mental insulators. This is because that "little voice" is sometimes for our good, and the important skill lies in knowing which part of that self talk is protecting you as opposed to undermining your confidence.

Never allow your "little voice" to go unanswered. Instead, give it space and listen. Then challenge it by asking it if what it is saying is really true and provable. If you feel that your "little voice" is making some positive sense, then take some time to rethink. It may be that on this occasion it is acting as your protector. The usual difference between that protective voice and the confidence knocking voice is, good reason. Some people are naturally skilled at differentiating between the two while others allow that voice to be in charge of their lives. The most important thing you can do whether you are skilled or not is listen, check those reasons and take notice of your levels of comfort with your decision. This thought management can be learned, and I would suggest that it is one of the most valuable skills to develop.

Mental insulators take conscious thought. We need to be aware of what we are thinking. This way we can effectively stop ourselves and call in whatever mental help we need. Other examples of mental insulators are mental affirmations which boost our confidence in ourselves and our goals and visualisations of success - seeing the end and what life will be like with that achievement in place. Mental rewards – telling yourself regularly what a great job you are doing is also a really good insulator. My personal favourite is a mixture of the physical and mental. When I see a piece of the goal falling into place, I am often seen standing up at my desk with a clenched fist in the air shouting "YES!" with glee.

Spiritual Insulators

Spiritual insulators can be described as deep inner strength. While the physical and mental strategies rely on conscious practical action, spiritual insulators spring from an inner ability for calm and balance. While the physical and mental insulators can be learned more quickly and put into effect immediately, spiritual insulators spring from more prolonged discipline and soul searching. They are the most challenging to learn but most rewarding in practice.

There isn't a book I have read, a course I have taken or a learned person I have met who hasn't suggested that the greatest route to spiritual awareness is through meditation and prayer. Learn to meditate and pray every day. This will help you to calm your mind and connect with your inner self with ever increasing ease and clarity. We all have a need to quieten the chatter and just create some spiritual space.

Everyday meditation matures our thinking and opens the windows of wonder so necessary to experience the joy of living while prayer is that heartfelt conversation and deep listening with our creator. For me, the latter provides a sustaining sense of belonging and connection not only with God but with those who have gone before me and who are now in his presence.

Despite the amount of media available on meditation techniques, I still meet a lot of people who feel that this practice is only for those centred humans who have some mysterious link with higher beings. Well, if you feel that way, let me dispel that notion right now. Everyone can meditate! Yes, meditation asks you to make time, to choose a conducive place and to be patient, all of which we have already learned to do through our physical and mental insulators.

The best advice I have ever come across is from a book entitled "*Ask And It Is Given*" by Esther and Jerry Hicks where you will learn the simplest method on meditation – relax and focus on your breathing. There are many opportunities to learn this invaluable practice in life. My advice is to go and learn.

Your life will be enhanced by the opening of that simply "being" space where wisdom resides.

Now that you have learned how to create the mindset for *The Rainbow Factor*, take some time to complete your Rainbow Factor Plan

Rainbow Factor Plan

Principle 1 – Authentic Mindset

My Chosen 3 Actions

-
-
-

Principle 2 - Live in Abundance

My Chosen 3 actions

-
-
-

Principle 3 – Believe you are Deserving

My 3 chosen actions

-
-
-

My Personal Commitments

I am choosing my *Personal Power Time*
My Time is from _____ to _____ each day.

I am creating my *Personal Power Space* at / in

_____

I am surrounding myself with those items which reflect my best memories or achievements and which give me most joy.

_____

_____

_____

_____

_____

I know my Power Insulators: They are -

My Physical Insulators

1, _____

2. _____

3. _____

My Mental Insulators

1. _____

2 _____

3 _____

My Spiritual Insulators

1. _____

2. _____

3. _____

You are now ready for the Rainbow Factor

Chapter 2

The Rainbow Factor

"Few will have the greatness to bend history itself, but each of us can work to change a small portion of events ... it is from numberless acts of courage and belief that human history is shaped"
~ Robert F. Kennedy 1925 - 1968

The Rainbow Factor is intended to be a regular practice to support the initiation, pursuance and achievement of your goals in an enjoyable and colourful way. I have chosen the analogy of the rainbow with its seven letters and colours as an accelerated learning tool which will help you remember the seven steps of the practice as well as associate each step with its own colour. Your potential to succeed is also enhanced by this practice as *The Rainbow Factor* is a whole brain process. This means that you can take advantage of your true and full potential to achieve your goals because *Rainbow Factor* thinking engages the left brain hemisphere with the letters RAINBOW, activating logical thinking, while simultaneously the seven colours engage the right hemisphere activating your imaginative and creative powers.

You will learn to automatically associate a word with a colour and a symbol for each of the seven steps. As you will now be using both sides of your brain to address your goal, your chances of success will be increased. If you simply make to-do lists you are only engaging half of your brain power, and thus limiting your abilities.

Therefore, *The Rainbow Factor* will always encompass – **word: colour: symbol.**

The Rainbow Factor
7 Steps to Life Engagement

Step 1 – Reflect: Red   Symbol

Step 2 – Assess: Orange   Symbol

Step 3 – Initiate: Yellow   Symbol

Step 4 – Name it: Green   Symbol

Step 5 – Believe: Blue   Symbol

Step 6 – Optimize: Indigo   Symbol

Step 7 – Work with focus: Violet   Symbol

The Importance of a well-stated goal

As you begin working with *The Rainbow Factor,* it is essential to know how to state your goal correctly. Any soccer player will tell you that to score a goal means getting the ball securely into the net, not near it or around it, but in it, so that there is no mistake that it's a score.

The same principle applies to our dreams and ambitions – we need to get our goals securely in the net so that there is no doubt what we are aiming to achieve.

Words are one of the greatest conditioners of our thinking. Our dialogue with ourselves and others is constantly forging our self concept and way of thinking. How we express ourselves and our dreams will help us to focus on our goals, or not. We need to line ourselves up right in front of the mouth of that net so that when we take our shot at that goal, we score.

Therefore in stating your goals, let's make sure of a few things -

1. **Own your goal** – it's yours so use "I". For example, "I am slim and healthy".

2. *State your goal in the present tense.* Remember your words condition your thinking so you want to imagine you are achieving your goal right now, not in the past or the future. Rather than say, I will learn how to play the fiddle, frame your desired outcome as if it were already attained: ***"I am a great fiddle player".***

3. **State your goal in its most successful version** – "the best / most fulfilling / most beautiful / most challenging....outcome, and choose a very clear and tangible word to describe that outcome. Examples are – *"I am the best fiddler I can be"* or *"I am enjoying a really fulfilling job"*, or *I am writing the best song I have ever written".*

4. **Choose a symbol to represent your goal visually.** Your symbol need only have meaning for you, but it should have a regular connection in your life and therefore be familiar.

A little help with choosing your symbols –

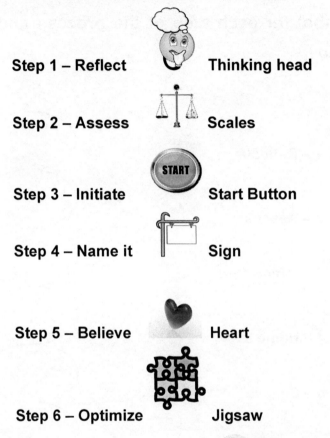

Step 1 – Reflect   Thinking head

Step 2 – Assess   Scales

Step 3 – Initiate   Start Button

Step 4 – Name it   Sign

Step 5 – Believe   Heart

Step 6 – Optimize   Jigsaw

Step 7 – Work with Focus   Target

Choose your *Rainbow Factor* Symbols- a symbol for each step of the process and draw it

Step 1 – Reflect

Step 2 – Assess

Step 3 – Initiate

Step 4 – Name it

Step 5 – Believe

Step 6 – Optimize

Step 7 – Work with Focus

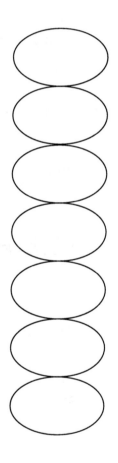

Chapter 3

The Rainbow Factor Working With Your Inner Coach

Once your goal is stated, you will need to check it out with the most important judge of all – YOU. You are the ultimate arbitrator in deciding whether what you are about to embark on is actually a good idea for your life. There are so many initiatives we can take in life that can on the surface look like at last we have hit the jackpot. However, if the fruits of achievement fall too short of the promise, it may be that the goal was in conflict with other aspects of our current life. We can be easily blinded by the outward appearance of our outcomes especially those that promise the solution in one tantalizing package.

I am not for a second suggesting that we take the magic out of that impulsive decision to just "have a go" in life, but sometimes it pays off to check out how we are going to live with that outcome. Will it actually fit into our lives? Now is the time to check the fit.

Always begin *The Rainbow Factor* process by having a conversation with your *inner coach*. Our inner coach is the voice of reason and in some ways our protector.

It can also be seen as a safety valve for the initiative or goal you are about to embark on. Therefore, before committing to action, answer four important questions:

1. *Do I want or do I need to do this?*
2. *Will the result enhance my life or the lives of others?*
3. *Is this the optimum time to do this?*
4. *Am I in agreement with myself on whatever my decision is?*

1. Do I want or do I need to do this?

If your answer is "yes", then you are pointing yourself in the direction of the net. The use of the terms "want" and "need" are important here depending on the goal. Some goals are discretionary in nature and may represent the "toppings" or luxuries of life, but they do not play a significant role in our development. They are by nature not necessary for us to live fulfilled or worthwhile lives.

Firstly, let's look at some typical "want goals". These goals are more generally connected to our life preferences rather than our life imperatives. Although some would argue that exercising repeated preferences, in time creates behavioural habits that can become the outward signs of character. The choices I am speaking about here do not carry notable relevance or capacity for character building.

An example of a "want" goal could be the choice of place to live, what type of job to take up or whether to exercise every day. Whether you choose in favour or against these types of options in life, they are unlikely to make you the person you are. They will surely support you and even open up opportunities but success in these choices delivers a healthy portion of that stuff needed to tell "war stories" around camp fires, and can be dined over until we replace them with a new supply. Therefore, the first inner coach question in relation to these may be *"Do I want to do this?"* A simple yes or no will do!

When it comes to the "need goals" in our lives, these are the more foundational or substantive initiatives, the outcomes of which hold deeper significance for us and are an intrinsic part of our development as a person. These goals by their nature have significance in shaping our character and personality and are less connected to preference and far more to who we are. These are the "need goals".

Examples of "need goals" are connected to how we treat the people around us and contribute to or detract from their lives, how we respond to seeming injustice or inequality or whether we are willing to speak up for someone less able to speak for themselves. "Need goal" statements could be – "I am treating the people I work with equally" or "I am speaking up for what is right".

The outcomes of such choices as these carry implications for development of character and ultimately the kind of people we are or will be.

Then the inner coach question of "do I need to do this" is more applicable and effective. The response of yes or no in this case should be seen as a marker for our life learning and it is the reasoning behind the response that is the indicator or builder of character.

Whether we choose to say yes or no to this inner coach question will point to where we stand on the important issues of life when "need goals" are involved. Thus we will make the choice to act or not, and the ultimate fruits of our achievement become meaningfully embedded in our experience. These outcomes provide a filter for our future choices as well as laying down a legacy in the world.

2. Will doing this enhance my life or the lives of others?

The second question to the inner coach attributes value to the action and seeks to assess its impact on people. Again the response provides an indicator of whether the doing and outcome of the goal will be positive and enhancing to our lives and those of others. There are responsibilities associated with any goals that affect other people's lives. Our actions can afford or deny another person the ability to be their best if our goals inhibit their success. We see this regularly in organisations where good people are denied opportunity or the chance to show their abilities because of another person's ambitions.

On a world scale, we witness the effect that irresponsible action has on the lives of others. We see how individual lives, families, communities and whole countries or continents can be wrenched and torn apart by the inconsiderate action of even a minority.

The rule is that the greater your leadership role, personally or professionally, the greater the impact of your actions on other human beings. So whether you are the head of a family, the CEO of an organisation or the president of a country, this second inner coach question is essential in informing your decision to go ahead or not.

In this context, the scale of social, economic and environmental upheaval proves massively disproportionate to the action itself or the number of players engaged. Never doubt that the action of even one person has the power to utterly change the world for good or ill.

As renowned economists and bankers throw their hands in the air in a helpless effort to explain our economic demise, the question could be asked what if those who could have made a difference had just paused to consider how the indiscriminate squandering of global wealth and resources was going to affect our world. What if someone had asked whether their actions would have enhanced the lives of millions? The answer as they say is now history. Yet, to despair would in itself defeat the question because now we truly need to set our greatest ever goals for the good of all. We need to choose the most life enhancing solutions for all, realise that the only time is now, and that there is no other possible choice but to agree within our deepest selves that we will survive and thrive once again as a stronger and better global community. A community that is more aware than ever before in history, that there is always a case to answer in the wake of our actions. It is an even more sobering thought that in time to come generations will ask what we were doing. Did we not consider the outcome of our actions? Did we not choose goals that would have enhanced our lives rather than leave behind a legacy that will leave an everlasting scar on our earth. The response from our inner coach presents us with a decision to be made – to enhance life or not?

3. Is this the optimum time to do this?

The timing of our goals is crucial not only to their achievement but also to our enjoyment of the journey and the outcome. Too often, goals are sapped of their energy by poor timing. Choose the optimum time for your goal if at all possible. Be ready to begin if the time is right and have patience to wait if it is not. The challenge is in knowing when to start. Have a good look at your situation from the perspectives of time and resources.

Here is one way to help you know if the timing is right. Visualise your life as a beautiful house with at least four large rooms, each representing the four key areas of your life – physical, emotional, mental and spiritual. Each of these rooms is furnished with beautiful pieces of furniture representing your past achievements and realised ambitions. Each room should contain a large storage cupboard with the capacity to store the unfinished business of your life – those goals or activities you haven't been able to get to for one reason or another. Now pop each piece of unfinished business into an imaginary small box and place it in your imaginary cupboards.

Need to complete your book? Put that in the cupboard in your mental room storage cupboard, along with setting an appointment with a dietician and embarking on a healthier eating plan. Need to improve your diet? Put that goal in a box and put it in the cupboard in your physical room. Want to spend some time alone in the mountains? That can be stored in the spiritual room cupboard.

To check if the time is right to engage with a new goal, go first to your imaginary house, visualise your achievement and go to your cupboards. Check your level of unfinished business. If you can see more than three areas of unfinished business in your store, think again about this new goal.

Unless you are willing to consciously forego what is already stored, the time is not right for this goal. Instead, pop it in your little box and add it to the cupboard for engagement after you have taken out and achieved another goal – in other words addressed some aspect of your unfinished business.

This exercise will allow you to stop and consider your priorities and activate a more relevant or timely goal, while retaining your new initiative. It is simply stored until you once again visit that room in your house, go to your cupboard and choose it because the time is right. The principle is: *"our levels of effectiveness are in direct proportion to the levels of our unfinished business in life".* So remember, when it comes to the right time, *"always check the store before you add some more".*

Your imaginary house and cupboards can play a wonderful part in deciding if the time is right for you to engage in your next goal. This is because it represents your levels of achievement, and is also a clear indicator of the levels of unfinished business in each area of your life.

4. Am I in agreement with myself on setting this goal?
One of my all time favourite writers and teachers is Paulo Coelho. In *"By the River Piedra I Sat Down and Wept"* he suggests that we never do battle with

ourselves because we cannot win. To me this says it all when we consider the fourth and last question to our inner coach. If we are not in agreement with ourselves about the decision to engage or not with our goal, then we will set up an inner conflict between ourselves and our intentions, a battle, of course, that we can never win. We are all familiar with this idea and we have all been on that battlefield, the one where, indecision and anxiety surround the goal and incapacitate our efforts. This "will I or won't I" contention overshadows the fresh idea and beats it down to drudgery so that by the time we get to try it, our goal has grown stale.

Don't let this happen! Instead, come to an agreement with yourself. Go back to the three previous questions and if your predominant answers have been "no", accept this and agree with yourself to wait. Remember, you have lost nothing – this goal can be postponed until you are ready to pursue it. By that time, life may have changed to the extent that the very context of this goal has been transformed and the answers to all four inner coach questions will have changed to "yes".

Working *The Rainbow Factor* – some points to remember

1. ***Always start with step one in The Rainbow Factor and work from there.*** The reason for this is that "*reflection*", which is step one, is always the starting point for any goal in life. By reflecting on what we are about to do, we are opening ourselves to whatever experience or opportunities arise because we are becoming conscious of our plans and actions. Reflection serves to clarify our vision because it encourages us to stop, look and question our motivations and beliefs.

    The power of this first step is proven by the fact that we may at times not progress beyond it, and may knowingly abandon a goal on the basis of what we realise by reflection and how this initiative or action fits into our lives. The inner coach questions support this.

Reflection is therefore, always first and is followed in sequence by steps 2 through 7.

2. ***Once learned and practiced, The Rainbow Factor can become an unconscious way of life.*** In other words, it becomes a habit and thereby serves to eliminate the indecisiveness and agonizing which often precede our engagement with our goals. It can become a default position to which we go automatically when faced with a decision. All areas of our lives will benefit from our enhanced personal effectiveness and confidence to move forward.

   The Rainbow Factor creates bedrock for our reasoning because we have worked through a natural process of thinking and action from reflection through assessment of value, and compatibility in our lives, all the way through to putting the effort in and working at it. *The Rainbow Factor* is a significant personal development tool because it helps us step up to the plate and start making things happen in our lives.

We also benefit from the process because it helps us to not just do, but do the right things. Once our hands are on the steering wheel of our lives, we are in control and we can choose the direction, speed, and the stop off points on the highway. And of course there is nothing can match the sheer joy of knowing that we accompanied ourselves through some great achievements which were chosen, checked and executed by us personally.

3. *The Rainbow Factor is FUN!* As we practice and progress with this way of life, we become more and more relaxed with what the universe has in store for us. We become more accomplished at self observation as we sit back and watch our dreams unfold in front of our eyes, and we marvel at what we can achieve. I often find myself having a little private giggle as I notice the universe playing

little games and rearranging occurrences into better order than my wisdom would ever dictate. Then one day, the magic happens! I bump into the very person I needed to meet to progress my goal, I end up in the very place I needed to be and I have the very solution I was waiting for in order to complete the jigsaw. It never ceases to amaze me and I have every confidence that you will experience that same magic.

So let's begin..................

You are about to engage with the **7 steps of The Rainbow Factor** – your guide to life engagement. Please remember to position yourself by **creating the mindset** as described in Chapter 1

- **Create your power time** – choose your best time every day to focus on your goal or project. Remember everything you do needs to become a habit so that this process will become automatic. Whether your goal is personal or work related, specifying and sticking with your chosen power time is essential.

My Power Time is _____

- **Create your Power Space** – that location in your home, office or outdoors where you are surrounded by symbols of achievement and joy in your private life or work.

My Power Space is _____

I am surrounded by the following symbols of my achievements:

_____

_____

_____

- Decide and be conscious of your Insulators –
  those protectors against negative influences

My Insulators are

_____

_____

State Your Goal

(Use "I am / have the best ...."
mentioning the best possible outcome of what
you will achieve. For example, "I am enjoying a
really fulfilling new job", or "I am writing the best
song I have ever written", or "I am collecting a
first class honours degree".

_____

_____

I have checked my goal with my Inner Coach:

1. Do I want or do I need to do this? _____

2. Will doing this enhance my life or the lives of others? _____

3. Is this the optimum time to do this? _____

4. Am I in agreement with myself on this? _____

If No: I am letting loose this goal or I am storing it.

If Yes: Then I am engaging with *The Rainbow Factor*.

Frances enjoying one of her passions – the great
outdoors at Lough Key, West of Ireland.

My boxer dogs: Joxer, puppy Jessie and Juno
– my greatest de-stressors.

Frances writing in her cabin

Frances heading to her cabin to do some reading.

Rainbows at Niagra Falls – February 2009

Rainbows at Niagra Falls – February 2009

Enjoying sailing in the Ionian

A race to the finish on the Croatian coast.

Playing with boxers in the snow

Frances with her husband Liam – her greatest supporter.

The Rainbow Factor

7 Steps to Life Engagement

Step 1 – Reflect

Step 2 – Assess

Step 3 – Initiate

Step 4 – Name it

Step 5 – Believe

Step 6 – Optimize

Step 7 – Work with Focus

The Rainbow Factor
Step 1 Reflect

Validate Your
Decision

"I read and walked for miles at night along the beach, writing bad blank verse and searching endlessly for someone wonderful who would step out of the darkness and change my life. It never crossed my mind that that person could be me".
Anna Quindlin

The purpose of step1 is to validate your decision to engage, store or abandon this goal. The good news on this step is that you have already learned to practice its key aspects in chapter 3 by working with your inner coach questions.

You will remember these four questions dealt with whether you want or need to do this, whether engaging with this goal will enhance yours or other people's lives, whether the timing is right and whether you are now in agreement with yourself on the decision to go ahead or not.

Reflection is both a discipline and a habit and will thereby become a natural part of your daily life in practicing *The Rainbow Factor.*

Your guide to activating Step 1 – Reflect

Once you have identified and stated your goal, ask and answer your 4 inner coach questions from Chapter 2. Do I want or do I need to do this? Will it enhance mine or other people's lives? Is this the optimum time to do this? Am I in full agreement with myself on my decision to go ahead or not?

Based on your answers, make a decision to embark on this goal or not. If not, consider popping it into your imaginary store cupboard for later consideration. If this doesn't attract you, then perhaps you will want to lose this goal completely. If so, do it now and clear the space for other future more attractive goals. You will find this mental clearance both liberating and empowering as undecided goals generally hang around our consciousness suggesting failure because we didn't proceed with them. So let yourself off the hook and say out loud – "I choose to let go of this goal in favour of something better to come".

The Rainbow Factor
Step 2 Assess

Accommodating Your Outcome

"I made my own assessment of my life and I began to live it. That was freedom".
Fernando Flores

Now that you have decided to move ahead with the goal, you need to get to know it, and make it welcome in your life.

Step 2 helps you to keep track of how this goal is affecting your life on a daily basis and the practice of assessment will keep you conscious of how your goal is changing and developing as it moves closer to fruition.

Guide to activating Step 2 – Assess

1. Assess your passion for the outcome

This is the most important assessment you will make. The level of passion you have for the outcome of this goal will determine the level of effort you are going to put into achieving it. The success of a goal will ultimately come down to how much you really want this. So be careful of little things that can disguise your passion like something I call the "September syndrome". This is the time of year when it feels like we should all be starting something new. This is probably a legacy of our "back to school" days. Come September, a little switch goes on in our heads and we "need" to be starting something, be it a course, joining a gym or starting the famous diet. Beware of the September syndrome and wait a few weeks to see if you are still enthusiastic and passionate about starting something new. This little assessment will serve you well and it will help you to choose goals which you are really enthusiastic and passionate about.

When assessing your passion for the outcome, take a good look at the reasons behind wanting this outcome. Sometimes our motivations are coming from an external source such as other people. When assessing your reasons why, find where your influence to proceed is coming from. Is it coming from a friend or family member who with the best will in the world is pushing you towards this goal for their reasons rather than yours?

I have been working with individuals and groups for almost twenty years and I have met many people who are living out the unachieved goals of their parents or siblings. I have worked with teachers who became teachers because a parent always wanted to teach, or because that was what all the men in the family did. Or the mother who looked on with sheer joy as her children fought so ambitiously for their careers, yet, while being joyous for them, in her own heart she wept at never having followed her own dream of becoming an award winning hair stylist.

Equally so, I have worked with people who had a deep seated hunger for doing what they do because it is truly their own passion and they must live it. They are willing to move mountains to get to that outcome and enjoy the pleasure and the pain along the way.

Just make sure you know where that passion is coming from – your own heart and soul, or the unfortunate lost dreams of others.

2. Assess the impact

Assess the importance of this goal in your life by its level of impact. Will the outcome have small importance or impact and thereby make a minor difference in your life?
An example might be improving a skill which will make life a little easier.

Will the outcome carry significant impact and lead to more substantial difference?

An example might be learning to drive which could make quite a change as it may introduce a level of freedom you haven't had before.

Or will the outcome of this goal be life changing for you? Typical life changing goals can be adopting a healthier lifestyle through exercise, change of eating habits and developing a more stress free existence. Often a change of career can mean a very different life for some people as can moving to live in a different place.

However, please remember that as goals are purely personal, we cannot generalise about the impact an outcome can have on another person's life. A goal which has a small impact in your life may mean a tangible life change in someone else's. Your goals are your goals!

3. Accommodating the outcome.

Step 2 - *Assess* asks you to consider what changes you will need to make to accommodate the outcome of this goal in your life.

This may be from a time or financial perspective. Where you live may be up for consideration if your goal is connected to a new career or job. Your outcome may necessitate some very practical adjustments. Last year a friend of mine decided to create an organic garden at the back of her house. As she stood at her kitchen window, she realized that space for what she really wanted to do was going to be an issue.

Her heart sank as she felt the goal start to slip. However, a good assessment led her to setting up an arrangement with her neighbour to use some of her garden in exchange for a year-round supply of organic produce.

Therefore, Step 2 *Assess,* means step back and do just that – assess what you need to do to accommodate this outcome in your life. There is no end of examples of people who succeed because they assessed their outcomes. The Great Central British Railway almost fell foul to modern planning processes, but through the in-depth assessment and passion of a small group of railway enthusiasts, the railway is now a fully working testament to the great age of steam. They set the goal to restore this beautiful legacy of the steam age and achieved it because of their passion for steam and their clear assessment of what was involved in the project. However, there is an equal amount of stories of projects that are enthusiastically commenced but left sadly unfinished due to lack of forethought and assessment as to how the outcomes would ever become part of everyday life. These are evident in our own lives. The course started and not finished because the amount of homework was in excess of what could be accommodated while still rearing a family. The riding lessons not pursued as evidenced by the very expensive unused apparel in the wardrobe, the house extension still awaiting completion because of lack of funds.

Assess it and decide – remember there is always your storage cupboard.

The following are useful consideration points for engaging with *Step 2 Assess:*

Passion - how much and from where?

Time - how much and when?

Finance – how much and how?

Space – Where?

Skill – which ones?

Personal Commitment – do I have it?

Who – do I need help and is it available?

Remember, your level of effectiveness is in direct proportion to the level of unfinished business in your life. Engage with Step 2 – *Assess.*

The Rainbow Factor
Step 3 Initiate

Getting Started

"You don't have to be great to start but you have to start to be great". Zig Ziglar

Get yourself started! You have reflected and assessed; now it's time to make a start and Initiate your goal. My rule of thumb is that once I have gone through a good reflection, carried out my assessment and decided to go ahead, I will take some starting initiative towards my goal within twenty four hours. This may be a phone call, or a short "to do" list. When I was sixteen, my Dad bought me a book for my birthday called – *"Bring out the Magic in your Mind"* by Al Koran. This book had a major effect on my life and how I would address my goals from that time onwards.

One of the suggestions in the book was that once you decide on what you want, go and get something visible that is connected with that goal and keep it close to you to remind you of what it is you are striving for. The book went on to explain the crucial role that the right brain plays in helping us realize our goals in life. When I finished reading, I went straight out in search of something that would help me stay focused on a goal I had at the time. I wanted to own a classic Morris Minor car. I headed up hills and down dales in search of the famous Morris badge and found it in an old scrap yard on the side of a hill in the West of Ireland. I loved driving the two classic "moggies" I later owned and I still have that magic badge.

All initiatives start with visualization and are propelled onwards by manifestation. That badge was the start of my manifesting the goal.

Due to some new goals, I parted with my last Morris Minor four years ago. It was bought by a man for his eleven year old son who at a very young age had a huge passion for restoring old cars. The eleven year old ably hopped into the driver's seat, turned the key and drove this gentle warhorse in a dead straight line up onto the car carrier. No prizes for guessing where this young passion lay.

I initiated my career by following my dream and going to college to study Psychology and English literature – my passions in life. Of course I learned a lot about the human brain but what interested me most was what I could do with it.

Many years later, my husband and I met Brian Mayne, the author of *"Goal Mapping; the Practical Workbook"* who introduced us to the left and right brain goal maps which he has created to help people achieve their goals. From the time I was sixteen, I had naturally visualized my goals and their outcome, so much so, that often I would surprise myself with the result not really being aware of how I was using my right visual brain.

Brian Mayne's work on *Goal Mapping* put it all in perspective, and now, I not only initiate my goals by visualizing them, I know what I am doing and have become what Brian often refers to as a conscious creator.

Your right visual brain is the gateway to your subconscious mind and if you want to achieve your goals in life, you need to introduce them to your subconscious by visual initiative – go find something to hold that reminds you of your goal, draw pictures of your outcome, collect photos as you progress and keep that subconscious door open. Your subconscious will accept that what you are doing right now is what you want, and will support you in your efforts to succeed. So think of visualisation as a means of getting your subconscious mind on board.

Engage with Step 3 - Initiate by visualizing and then get out there and find some item that you can carry around with you to remind you of your goal.

Make the calls, write the notes, purchase the materials but most of all see yourself succeeding.

Step 3 lends energy to your goal activity and you will find that your goal will start to move and become a part of your daily activities. So strap in and get ready for the ride of your life!

Guide to Step 3 – Initiate

1. Activate your goal *within 24 hours* of your decision to go ahead with it.
2. Do a *Goal Map* – check out Brain Mayne's book – *"Goal Mapping – The Practical Workbook"* referenced at the back of this book.
3. *Visualize yourself succeeding* and having achieved your goal and involve your subconscious mind in your efforts.

4. Ensure that you *do something towards your goal every day* regardless of how small that action is – this will keep you moving towards your outcome.

5. *Stay Positive about what you are doing* and use your *Power Insulators* to protect you against negative influences.

The Rainbow Factor
Step 4 Name it

"What's the use of their having names the Gnat said, 'if they won't answer to them?' 'No use to them,' said Alice; 'but it's useful to the people who name them, I suppose".
Louis Carroll1832 - 1898)
Source: Through the Looking Glass and What Alice found.

Now that your goal is up and running, and some part of every day is dedicated to its achievement, the goal is gaining identity as part of your life.

Step 4 - *Name it,* gives your goal identity, and formalises its part in your everyday life. Just think about the difference your own name makes to you.
It serves to single you out and gets you attention, which is exactly what you want for your goal.

The moment you *Name* your goals, they become yours and that ownership strengthens and closes the gap between you and success. People in the marketing profession have known this for years and we all know the power of a name as it flashes by us on a motorway billboard or bursts across our T.V. screens. It never fails to grab our attention.

In fact, the marketing world makes such great use of the subconscious mind in creating those memorable product visuals that we spoke about in Step 3, that we are drawn towards those products to the exclusion of many others that do just the same thing. The secret is in the name – so *Name* that goal!

Choosing a name for your goal is fun, and let's face it, if there is one thing you want to do in achieving this goal is to enjoy the journey and have fun with it. Of course there may be difficult patches – my mind goes back to the day I sat exasperated looking at my first Morris Minor and particularly at the amount of rust treatment I had to do to keep old "Bessie" looking good. Ah, but when we hit the road and particularly the West Cork Morris Minor Rally, "Bessie" not only looked great but was known by name by other enthusiasts. Project "Bessie" was ongoing. So make choosing a name for your goal fun!!

How do you feel about your goal when you think about it? Does it remind you of something else in your life which gave you the same feeling or focus on the outcome? Give your goal a name based on that.

Our goal to sail in Greece became *"Greek Salad"* as that's what came to mind when we thought about the goal – we visualized our outcome as sitting in little bays in the Ionian Islands on the deck of our yacht eating Greek salad. When I was building up my profile as an international conference speaker, we always referred to it as *"project natter"* while the building of our coaching cabin became, and still is affectionately referred to as *"the little house on the prairie"* in memory of a T.V. series we loved when we were children.

Other names I have come across are *"green fingers"* as a gardening project, *"project chill"* for a lady who set a goal on life balance. Choose a name that makes sense to you and makes you smile when you talk about it. Once your goal is named, it lives.

Guide to activating Step 4 – Name it

1. Look at the nature of your goal and choose a name that makes sense to you and makes you laugh – do this even for work related goals.
2. Make your goal part of regular conversations using its name. This attracts other people's attention and energy which can promote your goal even more. The name will often ignite curiosity, and curiosity is the natural home of good ideas – all needed for winning goals.
3. Keep your goal name visible – write it up where you will regularly see it and as we mentioned before, illustrate it. This will keep the goal firmly stitched into your everyday life and enhance your potential to succeed by whole brain involvement. *Goal Mapping* is wonderful for this.

The Rainbow Factor
Step 5 Believe

"One person with a belief is equal to a force of ninety-nine who have only interests".
John Stuart Mill

Steps 1 through 4 are practical in nature and can be activated by your passion, resolve and commitment to your goal. Step 5 – *Believe,* is different because it relies on an already present belief in yourself and what you are setting out to do. Belief doesn't switch on and off. It is the product of time spent in proving to ourselves that we are capable of success and the personal skills of dealing with challenges while not allowing them to erode our self confidence.

People who believe in themselves have worked to get to this stage. It may well be that this goal you have set will be the one that will teach you self belief.

It may happen that as you experience the ups and downs of pursuing your goal that you will use the "ups" to consolidate your self-belief in your abilities and the "downs" to adjust and restart. This will give you the opportunity to tend to your self-belief while you work to achieve your goal.

There is a great lesson to learn in the development of self-belief – just because you may not achieve the outcome you've planned, it doesn't always mean that you couldn't do it.

Remember all that stuff about choice and timing of goals? – if you don't reach your desired outcome, it could just mean that this goal was the wrong one, at the wrong time in the wrong place. Therefore, it is very important to separate your self-belief from your goal belief in order to survive the "downs".

None of us are strangers to disappointment. However, managing disappointment is an important part of living, especially when we realise the power of the word itself. If we work on this term and break it up into its component parts, we can de-power its ability to shake our confidence. One of the really cool things I learned about sailing a big yacht is that when you take the power out or "de-power" the mainsail – everything slows down. Even on the windiest day – de-power and you are more in control. There is no doubt but that disappointment can take the wind out of our sails and we have empowered this word even more by the level of emotion we attach to it.

We can "de-power" that word – "disappointment" just as we can de-power that mainsail. Just split it up into its component parts. All that "dis–appointment" means is that an appointment with your goal has been cancelled or maybe postponed. It is undone for now and that is it, and if we can avoid the emotional attachment we further "de-power" and we regain control.

Your belief in yourself is only threatened when you mis-manage your dis-appointment when not reaching your desired outcome. Remember, your belief in yourself and your belief in the goal are two separate things which only mis-managed dis-appointment can bring together.

Move on and avoid the emotion by bypassing the "I told you so chat" and remind yourself that your self-belief is off limits to the downs of disappointment. At the end of this section, you will find a very effective visualisation exercise which will help you to make this separation.

Guide to activating Step 5 - Believe

1. In your mind, firmly separate self-belief from goal-belief – your self-belief is impervious to the downs of disappointment. In other words, it cannot be damaged by not achieving your planned outcome.

2. When you succeed, see this as a double win in that you have strengthened your self-belief and also achieved your desired outcome.

3. If you do not succeed with your goal, manage your "dis-appointment" by seeing this goal as one

that may have been untimely or poorly chosen, and let it go!

4. Following point 3, move swiftly on to your next goal with your self-belief in tact.

Visualisation Exercise for Separating Self-belief from Goal Belief

Once you have set your goal...

Close your eyes and imagine yourself standing tall with your goal in your arms. (choose the symbol you have chosen to visualize your goal for example, an academic goal could be represented by your graduation hat or scroll in your hands).

Now imagine yourself placing that goal symbol on a table beside you saying 3 times aloud –"I believe in this goal".

Now walk to the other side of the room leaving your goal behind you.

Stand tall on this other side of the room and say aloud 3 times –"I believe in me".

Open your eyes and do the same exercise that you have visualized, physically. You can repeat this exercise as often as you wish and it will help create a tangible separation in your mind between your self-belief and your goal-belief.

Think about your life and the number of times that perceived failure has taken the wind out of your self-belief, de-powering you, and discouraging you from trying again.

You did not separate you from your goal, and when the goal got into bother, so did you. The world has a nasty habit of labelling us according to our achievements and unfortunately also according to our failures. By creating that gap, we open up the space of objectivity which allows us to see that we just haven't pulled it off this time and we muster the self-belief to try again because we are who we are, not what we do.

The Rainbow Factor
Step 6 Optimize

"What matters is not the length of the wand but the magic in the stick." Anonymous

O.K. now it's time to put the best of what you have to work – to optimize your skills and abilities to achieve this goal. Optimizing skills and abilities is only possible when you know what they are and how to match them against the goal. Of all the resources you may have available to you, the most important will be as mentioned before, your passion for what you are doing. This will fuel everything else and will in itself increase significantly your potential to succeed. When it comes to optimizing your resources, regardless of how accomplished you are, you will be underpowered if you lack passion for the outcome.

However, life often imposes goals upon us for which we do not have a driving ambition. Optimizing for these goals may be reliant on pure willpower and discipline and not passion.

What to do? Well you could try to strip these goals down until you find some aspect that inflames your passion, and optimize based on that. I have never met anyone who could really hide their dispassion for something they were unhappy doing. Some aspect of their personality, words or behaviour, inevitably betray their efforts at pretence. We spoke at the early stages of this book about the importance of living an authentic life. Pretence can never find a home with authenticity. So how can we live that life and still do what we have to do even when we are dispassionate about it?

Search for the little aspect that even only mildly attracts you and *Optimize* on that. When asked if you are enjoying what you are doing, answer with this aspect in mind. In conversation about the potential for success, think and talk from the context of this aspect and when you are in the throws of trying to survive the demands of a dispassionate job, focus on that aspect.

How many times have you heard people say that they stay in a job because of the people, and every work related conversation they have is centred on those people? How many people commit to being involved for a set period of time doing a task that does not make their hearts sing, yet they focus on the one positive aspect for them and it gets them through. The secret is to consciously make the choice, the agreement with yourself and do what you have agreed to do. You cannot optimise that which you despise doing as it has nothing to give to you.

However, you can choose that small angle or activity from which you can extract enough power to survive. But only if you consciously choose!

For a really successful Step 6, you need to be operating from a place of authentic passion and love for what you are doing.

The goal must bring out the best in you so that you can *Optimize* it.

From this position you will match your best personal and professional strengths with this goal and this optimization will hugely enhance your success.

Guide to activating Step 6 – Optimise

1. Find your passion in the goal and state it – "in this goal I am passionate about"...

2. Brainstorm the goal to ascertain what it needs in order to succeed – what resources, skills, abilities and personality.

3. Do an inventory of what you have got personally to support you in achieving your outcome. Consider from whom and where you will access the balance.

4. Keep reminding yourself why you are doing this – even if that reason is only a small part of the big picture.

5. If you lack passion for this goal, yet it has to be addressed, find someone to help you who has

the passion to follow it through to the end. This way you optimize their contribution.

The Rainbow Factor
Step 7
Work with Focus

"The difference between try and triumph is a little umph." Author Unknown

Every goal needs work, even those we are most passionate about. Though popular psychology might suggest that the universe is everybody's workhorse these days, we need to take responsibility and be actively and positively engaged for our goals to move forward. My experience has been that the more I move towards achievement, the more the universe co-operates by delivering those quirky opportunities and solutions that for some reason are exactly what I need at exactly the right time. There is power in action and work energizes your goal.

However, work without focus will sap your energy and you will tire of your goal even if you are passionate about it. If the path to your desired outcome becomes a maze, you will use up your energy and resources trying to find your way, as opposed to focusing on the direct path to your reward – the achievement. The goal becomes too hard and the passion subsides.

Step 7 – *Work with Focus* helps you to work with direction and objective. It will also help you to keep your path as clear as possible so that when you reach your outcome, you have the energy to experience the joy and celebrate the achievement. Too often I have worked with clients who have achieved enormous outcomes in their personal and professional lives, but at the expense of their ability to enjoy the reward. They buried themselves in a flurry of unfocused activity of doing, redoing and undoing coupled with the anxiety of such an existence.

In most cases, someone else had the pleasure of enjoying the reward which was meant to be shared. The final step in *The Rainbow Factor* is all about preventing that happening to you, and is a culmination of all the other steps that you have already worked through.

The keys to Step 7 – *Work with Focus* are personal organisation and the ability to focus on your outcome, along with knowing when you need help.

There are a lot of us out there who love control and derive a strong sense of satisfaction from making sure our hand has been on every aspect of what we are doing. We need to take that modern day proverb seriously and "get a life".

Achieving the goal doesn't always mean we have to do everything. To Work with Focus we need to employ Steps 1 through 6 and add that last "umph" which is the difference between try and triumph. You want to emerge from your goal energized and with the sense that it has all been worth it.

Guide to activating Step 7 – Work with Focus

1. Have a plan – again I say, *Goal Map* your goal.
2. Start every morning with a positive thought about your goal.
3. Commit to taking one step however large or small toward your desired outcome every day – this means plan your time.
4. Track your progress – write down what is changing and don't forget to illustrate your success and of course celebrate as you progress.
5. When you feel you may be getting distracted, ask yourself if what you are doing now is taking you in the direction of your outcome? If not – cut it loose.
6. Speak positively about your goal and smile when you talk about it.
7. Plan what you are going to do when you succeed and think about this every day.
8. Be grateful for the power to think, plan and work with focus on your goal.

9. Keep your eye on the universe – stay aligned with opportunity.

10. Know that your Self-belief and your Goal-Belief are two separate entities only destined to meet on achievement.

11. Enjoy the Journey!

12. Be comfortable taking the credit.

Conclusion

The Rainbow Factor Key Learning Points

When using *The Rainbow Factor,* always think "RAINBOW" and for each letter visualise its equivalent colour and choose your personal symbol to help you keep focused on this step in achieving your goal.

The Rainbow Factor – 7 Steps to Life Engagement

Step 1 – Reflect: Validate your goal by taking the time to do your advanced thinking and answer your 4 inner coach questions. State your goal in personal and present terms.

Step 2 – Assess: Consider the impact of your desired outcome on your life. Check out the level of impact and what you will have to do to accommodate the change.

Step 3 – Initiate: Make a start! Set out to begin within 24 hours of choosing to engage with your goal.

Step 4 – Name it: Choose a name that will give identity and secure your personal ownership with your goal – make it fun!

Step 5 – Believe: Remember to separate your Self-Belief from your Goal-Belief.

Step 6 – Optimize: Support your goal with all your strengths and talents and feel good about asking for help if you need it.

Step 7 – Work with Focus: Do something every day towards your goal and remember to keep visualising success.

"*I read and walked for miles at night along the beach, writing bad blank verse and searching endlessly for someone wonderful who would step out of the darkness and change my life. It never crossed my mind that that person could be me*".
Anna Quindlin

Frances Tolton is an international trainer, author and conference speaker. She is a *Goal Mapping* Master Practitioner and Passion Test Facilitator presenting seminars all over the world for those who wish to follow their dreams. She has appeared on primetime T.V. and is a regular contributor to Personal Development Programmes.

Frances also works as an executive coach to global blue-chip organisations assisting executives in realising their true leadership potential.

Find out more about inviting Frances to speak at your corporate or international event by checking out www.therainbowfactor.com or email Frances on frances@secondsighttraining.com

Other Life Engagement Reading

- ❖ *Goal Mapping – The Practical Workbook by Brian Mayne*
- ❖ *Life Mapping by Brian and Sangeeta Mayne*
- ❖ *The Power of Intention by Dr. Wayne Dyer*
- ❖ *Ask and it is Given by Esther and Jerry Hicks*
- ❖ *The Passion Test by Janet Bray Attwood & Chris Attwood*
- ❖ *The Seven Spiritual Laws of Success by Depak Chopra*
- ❖ *Bring out the Magic in your Mind by Al Koran*
- ❖ *By the River Piedra I sat Down and Wept by Paulo Coelho*
- ❖ *Meteorology Today – a text by Donald Ahrens*

Lightning Source UK Ltd.
Milton Keynes UK
16 April 2010

152906UK00001B/19/P